FOREWORD

Hello reader,

Art is all around us. We can experience art in all types of ways, from paintings and sculptures to fashion, music and dance. And it's not just limited to those traditional mediums like paint and canvas – anything can be turned into art, even people! I live my life as an artwork!

As you explore the works of different artists in this book, I encourage you to think about how you can create art too. Whether it's painting, drawing, sewing, sticking, collecting, or reusing and recycling materials, there are so many ways to express yourself through art.

I hope this book inspires you to discover the artist within you and create something truly amazing. Don't just look at art, create it – because you can! Use your creativity to make something that reflects who you are and what you care about.

Don't be afraid to experiment and try new ideas. The most important thing is to have fun and be proud of what you create.

Remember, be yourself – your uniqueness can make you the most unstoppable artist.

DANIEL LISMORE

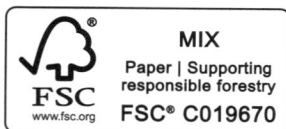

FSC
www.fsc.org

MIX
Paper | Supporting
responsible forestry
FSC® C019670

ISBN: 978-1-913339-37-1
Text copyright © Loll Kirby 2024
Illustrations copyright © Ruth Burrows 2024

Many thanks to the artists featured in this book for their approval.
Any unforeseen faults will be rectified for any future printings.

UNSTOPPABLE ARTISTS

Written by Loll Kirby

Illustrated by Ruth Burrows

First published in the UK
2024 by Owlet Press
www.owletpress.com

ART IS EVERYWHERE!

Art is everywhere — in our homes, our schools, and most importantly, inside all of us. Since time began, we've been expressing ourselves through art because it helps us to feel truly alive.

Art means something different to all of us, so when we talk about art — whether it's someone else's work or something we've made ourselves — it sparks ideas and conversations that help us see things from another point of view.

Understanding others as well as ourselves helps
us work together to solve problems and bring joy,
so creating art that gets people talking makes
the world a better place.

If we want to change the world we need to do things
differently, just like all the people in this book have done.
Times tables, grammar and other facts might be useful,
but let's look beyond what can be measured in a test.
Let's challenge what isn't fair, celebrate creativity and make
sure everyone has a say in what the future looks like.

This book brings together talented artists, throughout history
and the modern day, who all broke the mould in amazing ways.

PAINTING THE WORLD IN NEW COLOURS

Colour brings fun into our lives, encouraging us to see how rich and interesting life can be!
Have you ever wondered at all the different greens that can be found in leaves?
Or why your school uniform or favourite sports team's kit looks the way it does?
The artists on this page created a style different from the realistic paintings
of their time, using colour to create art unlike anything seen before.

Les FAUVES

Les Fauves were a group
of artists interested
in painting nature,
but in a more
unexpected way
than Impressionists
like Claude Monet, perhaps with
pink mountains or purple rivers.

They were keen to
explore how colours
worked together or
contrasted with each
other and what
effect this
had on us.

JACK COULTER

Jack Coulter's experience of living with synaesthesia can sometimes be overwhelming because he experiences colours intensely, even in his dreams. However, his ability to see music allows him to create abstract paintings based on songs, giving us an incredible new way to appreciate both art and music.

JOAN MITCHELL

Joan Mitchell used a wide range of colours throughout her life's work, choosing carefully to reflect the changing landscapes she saw and the memories she kept with her of places and moments that spoke to her soul. Colour was her way of showing us what she felt inside as she experienced the world around her.

USING SHAPES AND PATTERNS IN EXCITING WAYS

Art isn't just about painting pictures of landscapes or portraits. Shapes and patterns can be used to make powerful and exciting art too, as the people on this page have shown us. You can let your imagination run wild and make patterns anywhere and everywhere – on paper, on clothes, and even with lights! Next time you're outside, you could see how many patterns you can spot on leaves, seeds, or trees, because nature loves patterns as well!

Indigenous Aboriginal artists from Australia interpret their culture through the dots, lines and symbols in their work. People like Daniel Boyd, Kaylene Whiskey and Minnie Pwerle are all making groundbreaking art that reflects their history in a modern way, highlighting the prejudices they've experienced, as well as the rich beauty of their traditions.

YAYOI KUSAMA

Yayoi Kusama creates paintings and installations that are all visually linked by the use of dots.

She says making art has helped her cope with a difficult life and her work often features dots to symbolise the mystery of how small things can join up – in endless different ways – to become part of something bigger.

KEITH Haring

Keith Haring caught our attention with his fun, graffiti-style images. He printed his shapes and patterns – including his famous dancing figures – onto clothing so that anyone could buy and appreciate his art. He felt strongly about sharing his passion for social justice and wanted to make enough money to fund his other work, like creating art for hospitals and working with children.

TAKING ART TO THE STREETS

Why should art only be available to those with lots of money or art education? Why shouldn't everyone get to see art every day? These artists have taken this fight, creating artwork that represents everyone. They paint it onto walls and bridges instead of canvases for galleries and make sculptures for famous landmarks. They believe that art is for all of us to enjoy, wherever we are!

Morag Myerscough is passionate about using her work to bring communities together and creating art in public spaces that means something to everyone who sees it.

She believes that the people who use the buildings and outside spaces she transforms should help her decide which colours and patterns to use, so that her artwork can bring a smile to their faces, whenever they see it.

MORAG MYERSCOUGH

MARC
Quinn

Marc Quinn created a sculpture of fellow artist, Alison Lapper, that stood on the fourth plinth in Trafalgar Square for two years. It was the first time that the space on top of this column, seen by thousands of people every day, had been used to celebrate a disabled person and was a groundbreaking step towards a world that treats everyone equally.

BANKSY

Banksy is famous, even though no one knows his true identity. He uses graffiti as a form of activism and often includes certain images in his work, like rats, police officers and children, so that people will recognise that he's the artist. His art encourages us to challenge things that don't seem fair.

ELEVATING EVERYDAY OBJECTS

In the past, 'proper' art was thought to be paintings of special or unusual things, or people holding stiff, formal poses, but that doesn't reflect our everyday lives!

Over the last century or so, some artists have been brave enough to show how ordinary things could be just as beautiful and interesting. They wanted their work to help us see that art is everywhere!

Tracey EMIN

Tracey Emin uses her real-life experiences of love, relationships, sadness and loss. She believes that art is about being open and honest and has shared things that no other artist has – like her own bed!

JEFF KOONS

Jeff Koons made a famous sculpture in the shape of an enormous balloon dog, like those you might see at a birthday party!

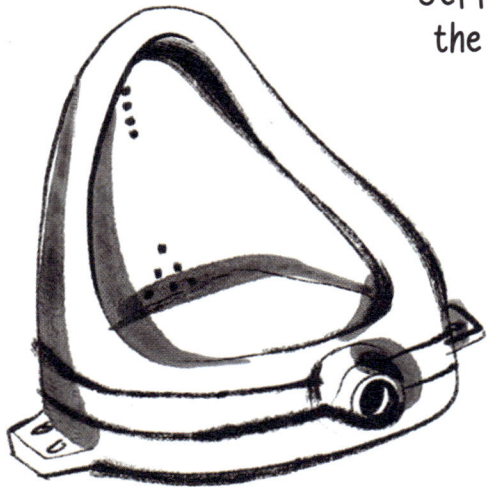

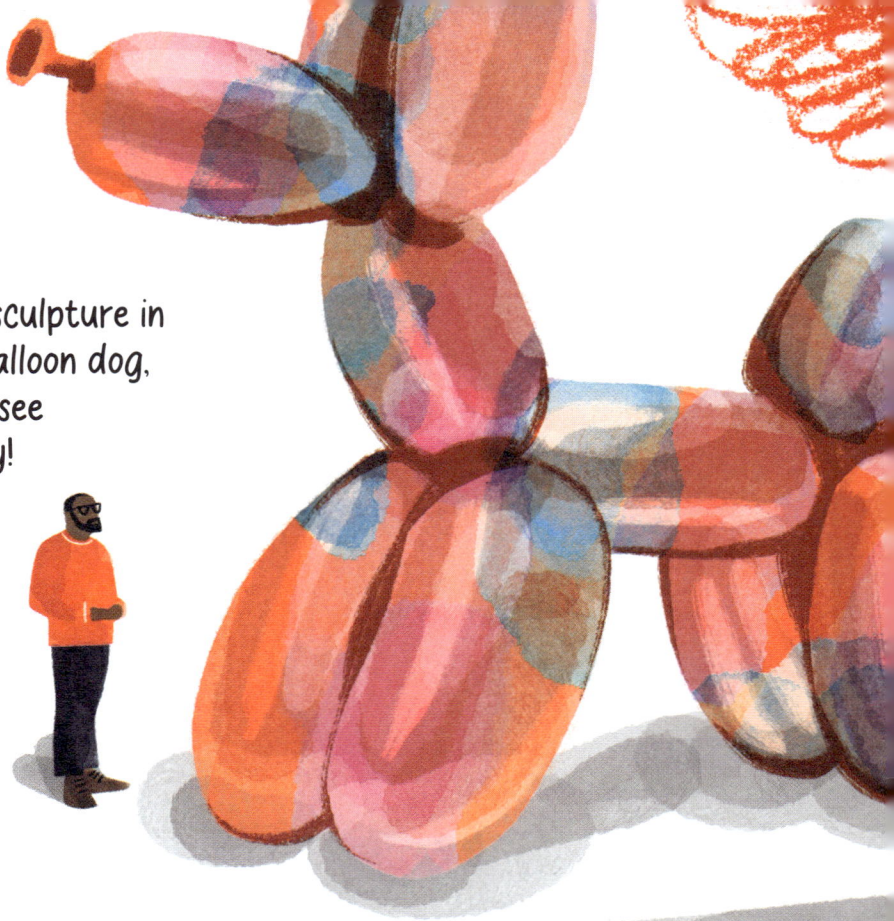

MARCEL DUCHAMP

Marcel Duchamp's 'Fountain' sculpture was actually a urinal that he put on display! Lots of people thought that was surreal – it definitely made them all stop and think!

DAMIEN HIRST

Damien Hirst was one of the Young British Artists: a group who shocked people with what they created. He focuses on life and death because people have always been afraid to discuss this openly, so he hopes his art will help us confront our fears and start talking.

BARBARA HEPWORTH

Barbara Hepworth's groundbreaking approach to hand-carved sculpture influenced many other artists, at a time when there weren't many female role models around.
She designed some of her sculptures outside as part of the surrounding landscape, showing us that art didn't just have to stay inside a gallery.

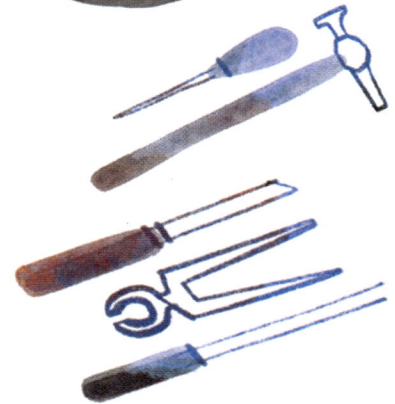

RACHEL Whiteread

Rachel Whiteread was the first woman to win the prestigious annual Turner Prize, with a cast she made of a life-size house! Her work stands out because she uses simple shapes, colours and lines. She's always wanted her art to mean something and for it to help us understand our everyday lives differently.

FEMALE CREATORS WITH NEW IDEAS

It's not easy to change something that's been the same way for a long time, but that's what these amazing women did! They challenged the idea that only men could study art or be successful artists and they created artwork in their own distinctive styles beyond the canvas. They showed us that women's creativity was just as valuable and important as men's, because we're all equal.

EVE ARNOLD

Eve Arnold took pictures to help us see the human side of famous people like Queen Elizabeth II and Marilyn Monroe and to give a fresh perspective on events like the Black Power and Civil Rights movements. She kept her photographs as natural as possible because she thought real life moments were the most important.

ANNIE Leibovitz

Annie Leibovitz is best known for portrait photography, especially portraits of celebrities.

She spends plenty of time with people before taking any photographs and is constantly trying new techniques, so that she can do their story justice with a single image.

AGNES DENES

Agnes Denes wants us to see the connections between the natural world and the world humans have built. One way she demonstrated this was by planting a huge field of wheat in downtown New York, so people could see the stalks growing, with the skyscrapers behind them, which caught commuters by surprise!

Sam VAN AKEN

Sam Van Aken experimented by making art, science and nature work together.
He created a single tree that grew forty different fruits! He included old varieties of fruit that aren't really grown any more to make us think about the importance of biodiversity.

Richard LONG

Richard Long is a land artist whose work in nature has influenced Goldsworthy and many others.

CREATING ART WITH NATURE

Have you ever wanted to make art, but just couldn't find any paint or brushes or space to get creative? These artists throw out the rule book and overcome problems like that by making art outside, with things like sticks, stones and snow! Their sculptures might disappear once wind, rain or curious animals come along, but working with nature reminds us how important it is to respect, and take care of, our planet.

Andy Goldsworthy's sculptures and photographs vary depending on the weather, the season, and the landscape he's exploring. His art is often designed to last for just a short time because he wants to show us that nature is ever-changing.

ANDY GOLDSWORTHY

TURNING OUR OWN BODIES INTO ART

We don't always think about using our own bodies as a place to create artwork, but these artists showed the world that we can change that, using themselves as their canvas! It might be an outfit for a show, or becoming a new character for a photograph, or it might even be painting on ourselves – whatever you decide, your body can be your own canvas!

BOY GEORGE

Boy George is a singer, songwriter, DJ and fashion designer, whose gender-fluid style has influenced many people since the 1980s. He's explored lots of different looks in his lifetime and continues to explore how art, fashion and music can express who we are.

Cindy SHERMAN

Cindy Sherman uses her own face and body to create artworks. She studies people closely for a while to really understand them, then uses costumes, make-up and props to build up her images, which she often uses to question society's expectations of women.

LEIGH Bowery & DANIEL LISMORE

Leigh Bowery and Daniel Lismore show us how bodies and clothes can become moving works of art, and that how we look is a great way to express who we are inside. Leigh used wigs, make-up and accessories in his extravagant designs and Daniel incorporates vintage material, charity shop finds and even litter into the flamboyant outfits he wears every day.

BUILDING ART INTO ARCHITECTURE

We all need buildings to live, work and have fun in, but who decides how they should look? Architects traditionally base their designs on space, light and the right number of rooms, but these architects took it to the next level and turned them into pieces of art as well. We might not know if we're looking at a sculpture or a stadium, but figuring it out is the fun part!

Antoni Gaudí was a Spanish architect whose style was unlike anything that had come before. His work was inspired by patterns he found in nature and his buildings were so unusual that no one could find the words to describe them. People still flock to see these incredible buildings today even though one of them is still under construction, nearly 140 years after it was started!

ANTONI GAUDI

FRANK LLOYD WRIGHT

Frank Lloyd Wright is a founder of modern architecture,

He changed people's ideas about how buildings are designed and used.

FRANK Gehry

Frank Gehry wanted the buildings he designed to tell stories about the time and place in which they were created, but also be interesting enough to last for many years into the future. He particularly enjoyed working on his family home, deconstructing an old house and putting it back together in a way that made neighbours gasp!

Zaha HADID

Zaha Hadid has been called the 'queen of the curve' for the way she used flowing shapes, spaces and lines in the buildings she designed.

Her designs are welcoming, as well as functional, with a focus on how people respond to buildings and she modernised many aspects of architecture.

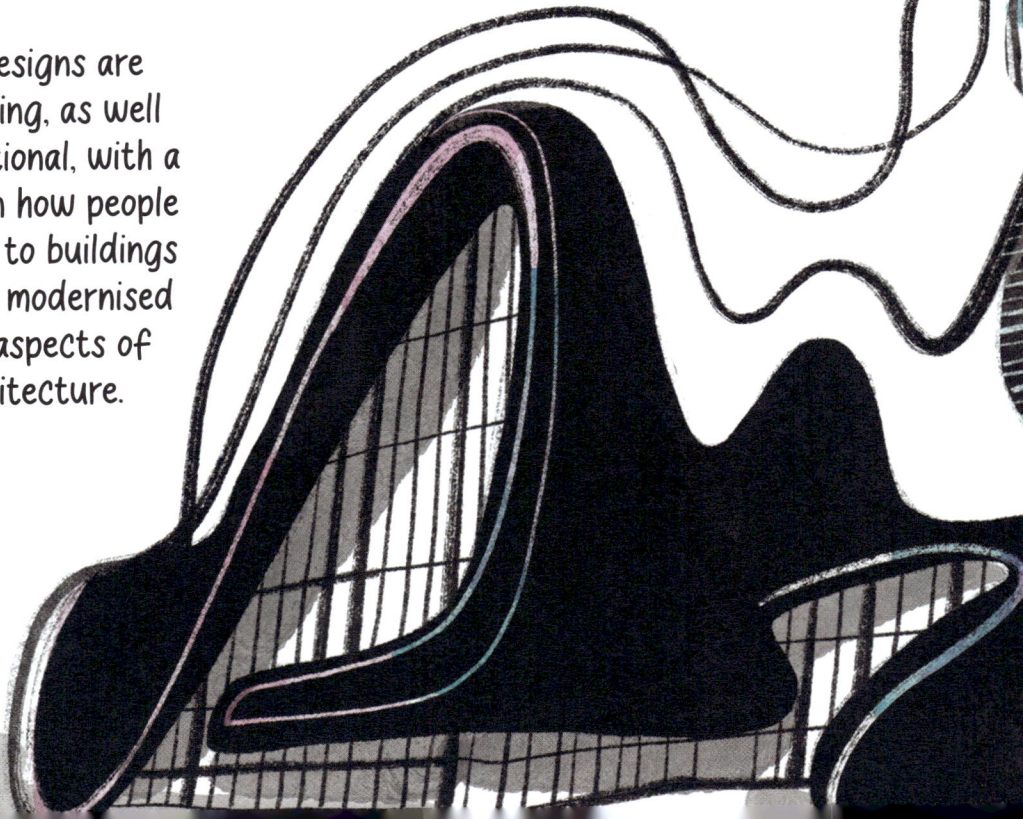

TRANSFORMING FASHION INTO ART

These artists took clothes beyond the practical and showed us that they're a way to share our creativity, choosing colours, fabrics, and designs that reflect our personalities. We can rise above trends and stop following the crowd, instead using fashion to express who we are and make statements to the world about what we believe in!

Les Sapeurs

Les Sapeurs are part of a movement called SAPE which is particularly popular in two neighbouring African countries called the Republic of the Congo and the Democratic Republic of the Congo. Influenced by dandies and elegant French tailoring from days gone by, Sapeurs wear brightly coloured suits with hats and other accessories. This challenges people's expectations by bringing joy to their lives even in difficult circumstances.

FALSE FACE

Jym Davis (also known as False Face) is inspired by ancient folklore to create masks that help people transform themselves into characters in their own mythical stories, set in new and unusual worlds.

Yinka SHONIBARE

Yinka Shonibare uses art to get us thinking about identity and who gets to decide where we belong. The British-Nigerian artist often uses Dutch wax fabric, a material commonly associated with Africa, as a central part of his creations. He helps us question what it truly means to be a citizen of the world.

ART IN THE PAGES OF BOOKS

You might recognise the work of these artists more than any of the others we've introduced because their work can be found on the pages of children's books. The artwork in children's books is just as important as the words we read and often shows us new and different parts of the story. Books are a wonderful way to take us to new places, but they're also a way of us seeing ourselves, so we need illustrations that bring us alive with their magic!

Beatrix Potter

Beatrix Potter was passionate about nature and she used the illustrations in her books to share that passion with young children.

She knew that stories and pictures were a brilliant way to let people know how important it was to take care of the plants and animals around us and her art inspires us to do exactly that.

DAPO Adeola

Dapo Adeola is an author and illustrator who uses his work to start positive discussions about race and identity. One of the most prominent black illustrators in the United Kingdom, his characters and stories promote diversity and through his hard work, he supports and celebrates black illustrators and those from under-represented backgrounds – he knows that art should be for everyone.

James Mayhew uses artistic processes like painting and collage to create illustrations for books. He even paints live on stage with huge orchestras, in amazing concerts! He is also a pioneer for picture books to be more inclusive and was one of the first gay illustrators to create artwork which celebrates the love between two male characters in a children's picture book.

James MAYHEW

NOW IT'S YOUR TURN!

You've read about other artists and seen how
they broke the mould – so now it's YOUR turn!

Free yourself to create something that tells the world
who YOU are and what's important in your life.

There are no right or wrong answers when it comes
to expressing yourself and you don't have to have
any special skills or training to get started.

Don't let anyone tell you that art isn't important or that
it's only a hobby. Art is everywhere, made from anything,
and it can change the world.

Look back over these pages and be inspired to
break the mould in your own completely new way!

SO, RISE UP, MAKE ART, BREAK THE MOULD!